# BULLETPROOF

Matthew Murrey

Cover & interior design: Daniel Krawiec

ISBN 978-0-936481-30-2

Jacar Press
6617 Deerview Trail
Durham, NC 27712
www.jacarpress.com

**ACKNOWLEDGEMENTS**

Grateful acknowledgment is given to the editors who published these poems, sometimes in earlier versions or under different titles.

*Ascent*: "Shower, Storm, Shooting Stars"
*Bellingham Review*: "Kitty Hawk" and "Skies"
*Blue Mesa*: "Rimsky-Korsakov's Bus"
*Calliope*: "First Aid Training Film," "Shoot the Sky," and "Si's First Lost Tooth"
*The Ekphrastic Review*: "Bronze to Bronze"
*Escape Into Life*: "Child Sobbing at the Library"
*Laurel Review*: "Up to the Farmer's Wife"
*Margie*: "And the Grace"
*Midwest Quarterly*: "Dead Cow Farm"
*Mothering*: "Steam"
*North American Review*: "Slugs"
*Notre Dame Review*: "Isotopes"
*New Stone Circle*: "Pity"
*Poetry East*: "Donuts," "First Song," "Forty and Ten," "Goodbye Sixty-Nine," "The News," "Solids," and "Twist"
*Poets Reading the News*: "Powerball" and "Shadow of a Prayer"
*The Progressive*: "Bulletproof Vest," "The Exchange: Oaxaca, Mexico," "Fireflies," and "My Goya"
*Rattle*: "Box Turtles Fucking" and "Teeny Tiny"
*Redheaded Stepchild*: "Lucky You" and "The Arch"
*Rhino*: "62" and "Lonely Tombs"
*Rise Up Review*: "Gravitational Waves Observed"
*Sleet:* "T-Rex"
*Spillway*: "Those Dying of Radiation Never Knew"
*Tamaqua*: "Dark Glass" and "Mosquitos"
*Tar River Poetry*: ".38 Special," "Dead Horse," "In Praise of the Dead," and "Iron"
*Tinderbox*: "Coyotes"
*West Texas Literary Revie*w: "Snow"

"Child Sobbing at the Library" appeared in the anthology, *New Poetry From the Midwest 2014* (New American Press, 2015)
"Donuts" appeared in the anthology, *The Book of Donuts* (Terrapin Books, 2017)

## I

## II

# I

## .38 Special

Steady now.  Steady.
I line down the sight
and fire off five rounds
that ring my ears and the air,
but miss the paper target each time.
I swing the cylinder down,
slide out scorched casings,
and slip in five new slugs.
This time I sight higher and to the right.
*BAM!* A little black dot
opens on the target.
And again, and again.
Now it is real that I could turn
and kill someone, or
put the barrel in my mouth
and tumble into that black hole.
I'm holding death's hand
as killers and suicides have done
and—I hate to tell you—
its weight feels good
like a sack of coins, a bag of blood,
a book of history, a pound of meat.

## Bulletproof Vest

Because one time a gun
was pointed at his chest
when the man with shaky hands
dropped it and it went off,
making a hole through the wood shelves.
Because the second time
he didn't see anything,
but when he'd opened the register
felt something shoved
into his back and heard,
"All the fucking money
in the bag...now motherfucker...
or I'll fucking kill you."
I was just starting high school
when he started wearing the vest.
I'd help my father strap it on
over his T-shirt, and under
one of his flannel shirts
that he would slowly button up
before heading off to work
which wasn't any kind of job
worth losing your life for—
a bar in a bad neighborhood
where whiskey and beer
were the only drinks,
where cashing paychecks
was how most of the money was made.
But it was the job he did year
after year, and it paid for the roof
that covered me, the sandwich
in the sack that I carried to school,
and the clothes that I wore:
the T-shirt underneath,
and the shirt that buttoned all the way up
from my smooth belly, to my skinny neck.

## Shoot the Sky

First black socks,
then navy blue pants,
then a white button-down shirt...
suddenly, outside my window,
from the backyard
came the loud crack of gunshot.
I ran though the house
to the kitchen where my sisters
were staring out the back door.
There on the back steps my mother stood
strong and calm as bronze,
still pointing my father's revolver
at the targeted yellow sky.
Then he came up behind us,
pushing his way through
with his startled and sleepy face.
She just slowly turned and said,
"I don't know, Honey—
I just felt like shooting the gun."

## Pity

It's the hammer again
as Laszlo leaps an ordinary day
at St. Peter's in Rome,
leaps the balustrade
around Michelangelo's *Pietà*.
The graceful marble
of dead Christ's fingers,
of Mary's arm and face,
splinters and shatters
under Laszlo's fast hammer.
Tourists and the faithful
are made marble by the shock of it
while Laszlo's voice
bangs the air, "I'm Jesus Christ!
I'm Jesus Christ!"

Pity the mother
whose child is murdered.
Pity the artist
sending his handiwork
down the gauntlet of time.
Pity the crazy one
who hears God's voice
ringing his mouth like a bell.
And pity my father
who stood for hours to see the *Pietà*
at the World's Fair in 1965.
Pity him turning
from the news on TV
where a snapshot of Laszlo
is staring at nothing,
turning to me
his nine year old son, to say
"They ought to just take him out
and shoot him like a dog."

## Bronze to Bronze
—WWI Memorial, Jacksonville, Florida

Streaked black and green, he stands
a close crow-fly to the hospital where I was cast
into this weathered world. Naked,

young, metal, and muscular—wide
wings outstretched from his back—
he perches atop a huge globe of bronze

aswirl with torsos and limbs and pained
faces. World of war
underfoot, he's gazing up, as if to take

to the sky where kids claimed they'd heard
the *thwump, thwump* of his wings
at night above stormed and stardarked roofs.

As a kid I loved to look at him: his freakish
wings and green indifference to all
the years of standing, staring, solitude and rain.

Pity him, forever looking up, poised to fly
but never leaving—his feet
welded to a world of grief, bronze to bronze.

## 62

The doctor's fingers smelled like Camels.
The nurse yawned like a snake.
A hand snared my ankles and hoisted
me up—skinny, skinned rabbit ready
for the spit. I coughed and cried.
Cry baby. Light slapped my face.
Malice poked its head in the door,
said, "Well, well...look what we have here!"

## Goodbye Sixty-nine

Like dice. Like castaways.
Like mice. Like runaways.

A stripped wall. A blinded window.
We were waiting to open presents.
Our father was fiddling with his Bell and Howell.
Our mother clucked, "Smile,"
and clicked the shutter. Snapped

between sprayed jungles and a murdered King,
cities on fire and taped conspiracies,
the Tallahatchie and the St. John's rivers,
the West Bank and a gun to the head,
the boredom of rooms and the dust of the moon.

Adrift on the open sea do you sink or swim?
In a dust storm what's best, future or past?
Buried to your neck in dirt, where will you turn?

Smile. The girls refuse; the boy offers his face.
Black and white, stripped and scraped—
give us this day our gravel road,
our four lane highway, our leveled field.

## Those Dying of Radiation Never Knew

Truman's first memory was green
guffaws: two years old he toddles
behind a frog.  Each leap
cracks him up anew.
His grandmother marks
what an exceptional boy
little Harry is, full of the spirit
of mirth at the tender age of two.
God bless the child.  God bless the frog.

## Isotopes

Even McNamara—that tallier of bolts,
fuses, sorties and kills—loved
that cool October night he figured
might well be their last.

In the library, my son bends
over books, assigned to unravel the feints
and jabs of that near disaster: Cuba in the fall
that my mother was carrying me toward my time

on earth. It all came down
to two letters, the movement of ships,
and what was unknown (the nuclear missiles
were already there: aimed and armed).

"Answer the first letter; ignore the second,"
said Robert to Jack—a stroke of luck
amid brothers, suits, uniforms, and fools.
The clock ticks because it is a clock.

The bombs stay put because...
The atoms in each cool core
are set to be crushed; in darkness
they keep such lethal light and heat.

Big with me, my mother hung clothes
in the Florida sun, hot enough to dry them
in late October. I see her bending and standing,
pinning them to the line. How things hang.

And here I see my son turning pages,
taking notes: a kind of proof, even if
it's just plain, dumb luck—who has whose ear,
the stroke of a pen—how the chips do, or don't fall just so.

## The Falling

Every night the day's atrocities
on the local news: who vanished
walking home from school,
what was in the garbage bags,
how many times with a kitchen knife.

In August's grimy swelter I moved
to Chicago from a small Florida town.
On the El to work each day I'd sit
by a window and wonder, *Down there,*
*behind that door? In that empty lot?*
*That man squinting at the sky? The one*
*beside me coughing into his fist?*

In December the first snow, my first,
began early afternoon—so quiet
and graceful, like God falling apart—
and fell into evening. That night
on the news, everywhere the falling
snow: on the shoulders of a reporter
standing in an alley, and on the two cops
kneeling beside the body of a woman
found gagged and stabbed in the snow.

Next morning on the train I saw all
the familiar places smoothed over,
so altered. Mud and torn grass, gone;
trash in the streets, gone; stained
and buckled sidewalks gone—
all so lovely and unscathed
as if forgiven, blessed, changed.

## Bike Messenger's Last Drop

Fifteen stories above brake lights,
horns and clenched steering wheels,
keyboards are quiet, doors locked
and phones mute in their cradles.
I'm walking back to the elevators
with an envelope left in the hallway
for me—my final run of the day.
Half past five and I'm past ready
to be done, to go underground
for a noisy train, to join everyone
heading home for the night.
Then an elevator opens; two women
step off, pushing their metal carts
of buckets, mops, soap, and rags.
They're speaking a language I can't
place—Serbian or Ukrainian perhaps.
They nod to me, then one heads east,
one west, toward opposite ends of the hall.
Their conversation ends, cut off
by distance and the rattle
of their carts. Last bit of work
in hand, I ride the elevator down,
thinking of those women—
how they smiled and talked
with each other; how one patted
the other's arm as they parted.
Also I'm imagining all the trashcans,
dusty tables, coffee stains, toilets
and dropped Kleenex—the tasks
they will bend and kneel to;
how they were separated;
how we are silenced.

## The Exchange: Oaxaca, Mexico

> "...they placed them on some rather narrow stones which had been prepared as places for sacrifice, and with stone knives they sawed open their chests and drew out their palpitating hearts..."
>
> —Bernal Díaz del Castillo
> *The Discovery and Conquest of Mexico*

It is a simple story:
I'm in Mexico drinking
hot milk with coffee
when a girl comes to my table
with gardenias to sell.
A simple story:
shoeless, maybe six years old,
she holds out her hand,
"Please buy it, mister"—
fifty pesos (not even a dime)
for one gardenia which I buy.
The meeting, the exchange
the terms for peace.
At this table in the plaza.
In the surf of that first island,
Columbus' trinity of ships
anchored against the sky.
At the gates of Tenochtitlán—
Montezuma trying to appease Cortés
with a moon made of silver
and a sun of hammered gold—just enough
to keep his hot greed glowing.
It is a simple story:
in my hand money,
in hers a flower.
White handprints of death on doors,
hands brown as coffee with milk,
the bitter and the sweet.
It is a story of looks exchanged
there in the plaza:
my eyes blue as the horizon

of the sixteenth century,
her eyes black as the scalloped edge
of the stone knife held
ready to saw open the chest.
A simple story:
one white gardenia bought,
and the living rose beneath my ribs,
beating and beating—scathed, unscathed.

## Dead Cow Farm

Here are the sad-eyed
plodding to the fence;
they hang their heads.
Destiny hangs on them
like a copper bell, pulls
like a ring in the nose.
Their big bones,
their silence, their faces,
make you think of recruits.
Make you think of war—
or dinner—don't they?
That's what you want to ignore.
That's what evolution's
been eating toward.
Offer your hand.
What do their tongues
and lips feel like?
I think *birth* or *naked.*
Come let's walk among them
like God in the garden,
like Judas during dinner.
I think they will trust us
as they trust the food
that fattens them, as they
trust the men who bring it.

## Dark Glass

One hundred and thirty miles paves out
before us in the flat dark.
After a day of the zoo, the Field Museum,
the shadows of skyscrapers—
we head south to leave Chicago.
I drive the interstate—a gulch
through rows of ugly high-rise public housing,
row houses, and low-slung shopping centers.
I drive the crush of traffic, red tail and brake lights
until 95th street when the highway splits
and spills the cars east and south.
One hundred and thirty miles to home—
my four year old and my two year old,
diapered and covered, are strapped in their seats.
Sucking their bottles, they're quiet, falling asleep.
It is 1995. I am their father, thirty-two years old.
We're in a used car, an eighty-seven Ford station wagon.
It's sturdy, but old—has nearly a hundred thousand miles on it.
I'll drive the two and a half hours through the night
without stopping once. I'll listen to the radio
for anything to keep me awake: tonight baseball from Denver.
I'll look over my shoulder four or five times
to check on two year old Gabe slumped in his seat behind me.
I'll reach over and touch my Silas' knee
or prop his head back up on his seat.
They sleep; they trust their father and this old car.
I'll track the little towns: Monee, Peotone, Chebanse,
Clifton, Gilman, Paxton, Rantoul:
each a dot closer on the map to home. But
always at the edge is my worry of this old car breaking down:
how we will pull over in the dark,
how the other cars will keep whizzing by,
how I will put on the hazard lights,
how my boys will stir and wake up,
"Are we home? Are we home? Where are we, Daddy?"
I will reassure them, tell them
that everything's going to be all right,
that we're just going to sit tight until a police officer comes.
I'll tell them that everything's fine, that we're safe and cozy.
That's what I'll do, sitting on the shoulder of Interstate 57
in the dark, 1995, waiting
for someone to come and rap on the dark glass.

## Dead Horse

A bat for the back
and the barrel, a stick
for the stifle and thigh,
a two-by-four for the flat,
long forehead. Whack,
thud, thwack, and thump.
Poll to hoof—with club, rope,
whip, or handle—I'll whale
on that beast, pummel
and pound until I'm dog tired,
until I can't see straight, until
the goddamn cows come home.

## Si's First Lost Tooth

It came out
with a bit of blood:
little lost bone
small as a tear,
shiny as a pearl,
painless as sleep.
Time's easy
with him now,
but a speck of blood
clings inside the hollow
of his tooth, sings
a red song there
where it joined the jawbone,
where the nerves lived.

**Mosquitos**

We'd be in the house at night
and hear it coming: a far-away drone.
Running out we'd listen
for the whine of the blower,
look for the flashing yellow light.
Soon my sister and I would spot
the small truck coming, trailing a great billow
of white vapor—cloud of poison.
As soon as it passed we'd run into the cloud,
play inside its acrid smell,
as the noise of the blower faded,
and the streetlight shined through the mist.
We were kids.  Mosquito larvae
like tiny question marks
stopped wriggling in gutters and sewers.
The fog of poison dissipated fast, so we played fast,
laughing and chasing each other
in the vapors—our eyes
watering a little as we breathed hard—
emptying and filling our lungs.

## And the Grace

The quiet of leaves letting go.
The quiet of a shovel opening the earth.
The quiet of granite, sunlight, and shadow
as I bicycle through St. Boniface Cemetery
on my way to work.
Beyond the far fence, traffic
bickers and creeps along, but here
the roads are quiet as memory, empty
as grief.
Rounding a bend,
I see five wild geese
walking swim-footed
across the cropped grave grass.
Quiet as cool air, I coast
closer for a look at these great birds.
Ten black-faced eyes
on question mark necks
watch my slow, rolling approach
until the nearest one shakes the silence
with clear, oboe-note calls.
They all rise, commotion
of honking and wings,
and find the way
of the air and the grace
of the season, then veer southeast
toward the beckoning fire bird's eye of the sun,
toward Lake Michigan's glinting
surface, skin of a dark hand
pointing that way. They
leave me to the quiet stealth
of red and yellow in the trees,
to the quiet of the wind's shifting northwest,
to the quiet of my kind laid fast in the earth.
They leave me straddling my bicycle
halfway from home, halfway to work,
my body wingless and wanting.

## Kitty Hawk

At the back of the contraption see
the soles of his leather shoes:
Orville's lying face-down flying
a few feet above the hard ground
which doesn't hold him anymore,
or snatch him right back.

The din of the engine,
the two huge propellers chopping the air
are so loud you can't hear
him whooping as he moves forward and rises
into the wind on the white cloth wings:
twelve airy seconds,
one hundred and twenty feet.

Off to the side Wilbur watches,
standing in his dark cap and suit—
a groundshadow of a man,
a lean counterpoint to all this lift.

The soles of a man's shoes,
his brother in a suit, the sand,
the wind, and the howling joy.
What will come, will come—and soon:
wingshadows above troops and trenches,
over borders, towns and crowded cities.
Messerschmitt, Zero,
Spitfire, Hellcat, Flying Fortress.

But first there is this moment:
a man in a suit, light of step
as his brother becomes bird,
dreaming wide awake that the world
is falling away from him
and that he can bring it gently back.

## The News

At the launch site in Florida
the whooping and clapping stopped,
stunned into silence or *Oh my God*—
hands frozen this far apart in disbelief.
Mesmerized, a boy in a classroom watched
the replays; so close to the TV
he saw his own face in the fireball.
On the west coast a man looked up
at a skyscraper falling towards him—
no, it was only the clouds moving.
In another country a table of men
drank wine to celebrate; "Goliath
tripping on his own sword," one said.
In Chicago, I was delivering packages,
about to enter a revolving door
when a woman took off her Walkman
and said to me, "The shuttle blew up."
I stopped and looked up, saw the usual
blue sky with a few roving clouds.
Nothing falling or failing, just a plane
high above the buildings heading down
west to the airport. All those believers
putting up trays, fastening seat belts,
probably still unaware of the big news.

## The Music

> "The hardest part is looking, quickly adjusting the distance on a scope, and then getting a steady position for a shot before he gets a shot off. For me, it's toning everything out in my head. It's like hearing classical music playing in my head."
>
> —Marine marksman quoted in *USA Today*, July 29, 2006

Like *Moonlight*
*Sonata.* Eye, finger,
trigger, the adagio.
In my scope a blur
of red where his head was.

I sleep soundly at night
because—wait,
in comes the counterpoint:
ah, light French horn,
and in my dream
a kettle drum opens
*Symphony Number One.*

Because I believe
in the beauty
of cross-hairs, of
every hair on every head,
that silence, that music.

I first heard those notes
when I was a boy:
pine cones and pop cans,
and my father shouldering
his M-16 to absorb the shock
as he talked me through,
as I squeezed the trigger.

The music would end
in a spray of splinters,
in a hole that let
the light pass through.

## Brukhonenko's Dog

Tubes move my blood. Close strike
of a hammer makes me blink.
Light shined shrinks my pupils.
Offered a chunk of cheese, I wolf
it down, though the gulped lump
soon slips from my severed esophagus.

World of wonders. The fortune-teller
looks you in the eye and says "Your nights
have room for more nightmares."

A president coughs; a general barks.
Tail wags dog. Tubes keep death tied
up for only so long. Sooner or later
in the crosshairs the living get dusted
while a minister mumbles, "God, it's dog
eat dog." And I thought I was your best friend.

## Lonely Tombs

Today while I slept
an army swept through a valley;
nearly a hundred were killed,
but not one soldier.
While I slept
my boy's hands grew large,
his voice deep,
and the world
threatened to eat him up.
While I was asleep
my dog peed the floor
like someone scared to death,
and somewhere a man
was being tortured with water
and somewhere a woman
was killed with a knife,
but there was nothing I could do,
so I slept soundly,
like my cat curled by my feet.
When I woke up
it was nearly midnight,
time for me to go to work.
Sleep had kidnapped my sons
and disappeared my neighbors.
Heading to my job,
I went along the streets;
they were lonely tombs.

## Give Them the Finger

Which one should you give up
if your kidnappers let you pick
before using the bolt cutters
or lopping shears? Finger
they'll send your loved ones
to show they mean business.

This was in the news the same day
NASA announced its Voyager 1
had left the solar system completely,
decades after leaving the Earth.

Not your pinky an occupational
therapist warned; you need it more
than you might think. Try hanging
from a bar and you'll understand.

I was in grade school when the probes
were launched at the far planets,
and endless space beyond. I loved
that scientists, so serious, sent messages
with them: maps, sounds, images.

I'm looking at my fingers;
I want to keep them all. I love
that those probes have escaped
with their little troves of music, photos,
and diagrams; with that plain engraving
of a man and a woman standing naked,
his hand raised *Hello*—open and empty.

## Up to the Farmer's Wife

He is a twisted man—
caught those three mice,
then scraped out their eyes
with his pocket knife.

Now they smell the meat
she's slicing for dinner.
He's not in—her feet
are the only ones they hear
shuffling around the kitchen.

Blind, they climb the counter
and crawl to where she's working.
Surely she'll pity them:
how thin they are, how grim
the scars where their eyes once were.

But we know what happens next:
three little bloody trails
crossing helter-skelter the kitchen floor
and by the meat, three raw tails.
That farmer and his wife, they are a pair.

## My Goya

With one hand I bend him
to my chest:
muscle, bone, blood, breath.
With the other,
I cradle and massage his feet—
two tense mice
whose tiny bones and pads of flesh
relax as they are caressed.
Soon my son's crying stops,
becomes the clock-like breath of rest.
It is when he is soothed,
and his feet are as supple as sleep
that I think of the Spaniards
rubbing the pads and heels with oil,
then bringing the fire.
I think of the Greeks
beating and beating and beating
the soles of their prisoners' feet
with rough slats of wood.
I think of the future
that holds us to his chest.
And I think of Goya's wild-eyed Saturn
holding the nude and headless torso
of his son—
the son he has murdered,
the son he is eating.

## First Aid Training Film

Looking up, he reaches for the bottle,
but the lid is loose
and hydrochloric acid splashes in his eyes.
He screams, grabs
at his face with his fingers as if it were a mask
he could peel off.
A coworker hurries to him, hustles him
to a showerhead in the lab
and forces his face up into cold water
spraying down.
There they stand, one man holding
the other as if
he were holding his own hurt lover.
Softly the rescuer speaks
to the one with the burning eyes, "It's okay.
You'll be all right.
I've called an ambulance; it's on the way."
Somewhere else
a man is pouring the burn into the eyes
of a screaming man.
"Where are they? Where are the others
you faggot piece of shit?"
But this is not interrogation; this
is first aid.
This is what a man can do.

## Gravitational Waves Observed

Nothing shifted here. It was cold.
Night fell. Overhead, Orion looked smaller
than he did sprawled on the horizon.

The fighter pilots didn't feel it,
dropping their payloads onto buildings
below. There is gravity, and there is *gravity*.

There is beauty in the dogged quest
to know—even if it doesn't save one life,
keep one boat from sinking beneath the waves.

In a thousand years there may be no one
to recall how men and women once were giddy
to have finally and accurately measured a millionth
of a millionth of a millionth of a meter-sized ripple in the sea

of spacetime. And what a time to be alive:
new particles revealed, a little probe hitching itself
forever to a comet, and ridiculously tiny waves arriving
a billion years after two huge black holes collided.

On Monday, it's back to work. On Tuesday
thousands will die, though far more will be born.
And every day the waves on the shore will break
the slightest bit higher than they did the day before.

**Who Now Will**

—after Las Vegas, October 1, 2017

paint flowers on the storefront check the straps on the car seat tune the guitar by the couch blow out all the candles drink Bloody Marys on Sunday make four lunches and bag them button his uniform and check the cells fill in for the teacher who is home sick tell jokes to the kids leave the night light on call the attendance office iron his shirt for homecoming set up a tent near the river go too fast on his four-wheeler shout for her daughter's volleyball team stomp a heel on the dance floor read another magazine about old cars call home when he's running late ask if she should take a little more off the top touch the diaper to see if it's wet sit with her in the doctor's office buy notebooks and pens in August text her when the show starts be her short dark-haired so-called twin help her roll her sleeping bag buy the plane tickets and reserve the rooms travel up the coast beside the sea pedal through the woods speed up the ramp and leave the ground make the slap shot that breaks the tie raise a glass for twenty-four years and almost one year of spending the night together get down on the floor to look for the chew toy drive to the college to take the GRE show them where to sit on the rug turn pages of the picture book let them sleep there when thunder booms take a selfie as the band comes out stop laying tile so he can sing "Man! I Feel Like a Woman" memorize their phone numbers tell them not to hit each other go to the library and read to them help him with his algebra cheer from the desert for the Steelers buy them milkshakes on Saturday make the pick on Netflix tonight explain how truckers stay awake sit staring up beneath pine trees stare at his breath in the flurries check the internet for the summer tour dates hum that line about being lonely show him the best escape and reverse spoon the pureed beans into her mouth teach them the stance and soft hands call you from work during lunch make sure she fills her pill dispenser right be honest about being shot at overseas get up early to make breakfast for four dance slowly holding you in close inflate the cuff and listen with the stethoscope read the history test out loud call the parents about the field trip buy nachos at Dodgers stadium stand outside while school buses unload ask the judge to rule on the motion practice the kick and strike in the mirror sweat through half-moon tree and standing bow snowboard on the first free weekend in February help the girl apologize for cussing out the teacher come back to ask who wants dessert face the camera for an hour under flashes and halogen lights spare the fly be the life of the party not have one mean bone hold on to a shockingly brave stranger's hand until there's no more strength in him to hold it and he has to let it go forever?

## Votive

I lit a candle in a little glass holder;
it glowed red and burned all alone
like the heart in its dark cathedral.
I lit it for the souls expelled from heaven,
exiled to this world where I live—city of sirens,
guns, and hustles, of barred windows
and bolted doors. I struck the match
and set the wick on fire for the spirits who broke
the laws of heaven, dared in His presence
to remember and mutter Earth's sorrows: "Oh
starvation, war, and torture." "Oh power,
greed, violence and murder…." To which God
barked, "The hell with you! Back you go."
I see them everywhere—sidewalks, trains,
subway stations; my candle burned hours
for them: the ones who stagger, whimper and bite
their lips, who stand alone talking to,
arguing with, and laughing at—nothing.

## Shadow of a Prayer

Thoughts and prayers are going
to do about as much good
as T-shirts or windbreakers would,
but a bowed head seems fitting—
I could do that. A raised hand
casting a silhouette on old siding
reminds me that—no matter
how solid I seem—light
shows us to be nothing
but shadows waiting to happen.
My turn's coming. I used to think
my chances for a peaceful end
were pretty good, that I'd go
like one of the old ones—in bed
mumbling and delirious in the room
where we slept for forty years,
or with family standing over me
as I let go of my last breath
in the same hospital where
I saw my son come into this world.
I can hope, but I'm guessing
the end won't draw such a circle.
Floods, fires, soldiers, famine,
bombers and cold-blooded men
with long guns and backpacks
stalk my nightmares. Prayers?
Go ahead; I won't mock you,
even if your first words are
"Dear Heavenly Father" or
you finish "in Jesus' name."
What do I got that's better—
my bitter thoughts, heavy
and grim as a box full of bullets?

## In Praise of the Dead

who do not do cruel things,
but lie there like Sunday sleepers.
They never say stupid things
like, "At least now he's at peace,"
and they let us do terrible things to them:
fill them with chemicals,
dress them like waiters,
stick them in narrow boxes.

I like how to themselves the dead are.
They don't brag about how much money
they had, or how beautiful they were.
And they don't keep telling you
who betrayed or disappointed them,
or how painful it was at the end—
how alone and afraid they really were.

# II

## First Song

There is a bird that started singing
at five in the morning,
in the dark at five in the morning
just as I started writing.
That's how I know
that it's spring, that I should keep
writing, that the darkness
has not swallowed us,
and that there will be morning
and noon and evening—a whole flock
of hours—although at this moment
in the dark there is just this
one bird, and no one
who can tell me its true name,
or why it is out there alone and singing.

**Teeny Tiny**

It took forever for the light
to fade. All my manhood,
that old overcoat, was gone,
and I was no more than five
setting off through the forest.

They say in a vacuum a feather
falls like a stone. They say
you see your life pass before you
when you're at death's door.
They say *jawbone walk*
*and jawbone talk.* They say
things I'll never understand.

I remember a story of a tiny boy
and his two older brothers lost
in the woods. They found shelter
for a night in the house of a stranger
who kept sharpening a long knife,
who kept calling up to the loft,
"Who is awake, and who is asleep?"

I couldn't stay awake forever.
Even here the feather finally lands
on the needled path, the heart
has a weight all its own,
and every step I take erases me
just a little more. See,
you can barely see me.
What I'm trying to tell you is
it wasn't a light at the end of a tunnel,
and it wasn't as scary as the scrape
of a knife being readied on a stone.
Then again, it wasn't a walk in the park either.

## Nailed

I'm seeing him before he died
walking in front of the house
where I grew up the same
house he and his brother stood
in front of their father behind them
his hands on their shoulders
as they stared into the camera
the summer after their mother
died in nineteen twenty-eight
when he was only seven years old
whilc in this memory I have
he's seventy-five and pushing
his red Craftsman mower
over the thick Florida grass
though my memory is no more
a memory than that old photo is
since I wasn't there but heard about it
from my mother who was also seventy-five
at the time and told me how my father
had been out front cutting grass
and had felt something pushing up
on his foot for five or ten minutes
which annoyed him though he ignored it
and just kept working which was
just the way he was but God
it just kept nagging him until
he finally looked down and saw
that he had a small strip of wood
like wall lath stuck to the bottom
of his shoe and it wouldn't come off
because it turned out it was nailed
through his shoe and into his foot
and he'd been walking on it
working it in for several minutes
the nerves in his legs and feet
having become so numb and dull
over the years that he didn't feel
the kind of pain most people would
but instead felt an irritating pressure
like a little stone in his shoe when really

it was a nail wedging its dirty point
right up into a bone in his foot
so the doctors had to cut up in there
to clean out the wound and worried
that he might lose the foot if infection
set into the bone and spread
but my father caught a break again
like the time the robber dropped
the gun and it went off on the floor
or the time my father lay in the crook
of a limb in an old pecan tree
and was chainsawing the branch above
so the blade was but a foot from his face
when it hit a knot and bounced out fast
but only glanced his ear or that time
the pressure cooker blew its lid
through the ceiling not ten minutes
after he'd been leaning over it cleaning
the exhaust fan or the time I watched him
pour gasoline from the can onto the coals
he'd already lit and how the fumes
made a gauzy white ghost of steam
that became a man-sized billow of flames
not two seconds after he'd pulled
the gas can away and set it on the ground
the memory I have is more like a dream
or a movie you forget then remember
words my mother told me on the phone
after she got back from the hospital
where my dad was staying overnight
so they could check his foot the next morning
for signs of infection or even gangrene
though it turned out he had neither
and he lived for another nine years
and I still see him walking the yard
slow and gimpy with that noisy old mower
and wearing his faded flannel shirt
and frowning mumbling and ignoring
a slat nailed to the sole of his shoe nailed
into the very flesh of his foot for Christ's sake
digging in a little deeper with every step
with every step digging right in to the bone.

## Shoot the Cat

That's what my father did: killed
the engine, went back in the house,
opened the drawer by the bed,
and picked up the loaded thirty-eight.

He'd been backing the SUV down
the driveway when he ran over Foma
who'd lived with my sister for ten years
before she moved to Rochester.

I'm not sure if it took two shots, or just one,
but if cats could talk, Foma would have
thanked him for not letting her writhe and yowl
with her crushed pelvis for the last hours

of her fifteen years in Jacksonville,
which had been pretty good up until that moment
when she didn't see or hear the Dodge Ramcharger,
and my father didn't see her in the wide mirror
at his elbow. They both were getting old.

## Snow

Almost, but not quite.
Quiet as a moth
against a lampshade, a sheet
being folded, the breath
of one you love. Still
breathing? Yes.
In my dream of the end
I walk such a hush,
every flake a minute
that has fallen away.
She says, "Winter is silence."
I reply, "Are you sure?"
Consider the second hand
going nowhere all the time,
a needle pulling thread,
scissors snipping at the edge,
lips parting, my hand patting
the lid three times, minutes
before the hired men
lower it in, cover it for good.
Finger to the lips: *shhhh.*

## Sheets

When I was little my mother
pinned them to the line;

the sun filled them with light,
and the wind rippled them

like white flags. So who surrenders—
the one at the door with a hand

on the switch to kill the lights,
or I on the table, shrouded

like a boat lost in a fog,
like a couch in a vacant house?

You there, on tip-toes at the window,
you're young enough not to

know better. Go home, and give
me some privacy. Don't tell

anyone what you've seen;
they don't believe in ghosts.

Tomorrow will be all yours;
take it, but remember me

when morning fog burns away,
when you see linens on a line,

when you get in bed and disappear
beneath your sheet.

## Shower, Storm, Shooting Stars

For the third time in my life
I got in a cold car,
and drove away from the lights
of town—twice for the Perseids,
and this time for the Leonids.
Each time I'd gone hoping
for something spectacular.
The first two were nothing
but a slow wheeling sky of stars—
this time, three faint streaks of light
in the half hour I lay on the hood of the car
trying to keep my neck loose,
trying to keep my backside warm.
It wasn't fireworks, or even fireflies.
It was just the beginning of dawn:
soft fade of light seeping up,
a fat, yellowed moon settling down,
and three shooting stars for luck.
Nothing to come home talking about,
nothing to remember on my deathbed—
unless dying turns out to be like lying
on the hood of a car in the cold,
staring up into the dark, hoping
for a dazzle of shooting stars.

## Child Sobbing at the Library

Suddenly the quiet, that empty jug,
is being filled
with crying. A child is sobbing: not the wailing
of a slapped kid,
and not the tearful screeching of demands
and whining. No,
it is a child crying for something lost
or broken, something
that will never be replaced.
I listen, loving
the sound, as I love a lone violin
or muted trumpet
slowly filling the bowl of silence.
It is the crying
that I've lost, and will never have
again. I want
that child to cry and cry for everything
I've lost, every love
I've squandered, everything I should've
done. Cry for
my deaf father sitting hunched
in front of his loud TV,
for the house on Kenmore Street, for the tea
we drank, falling in love,
for the novels I'll never read, for the great
paintings hanging unseen
all night in empty museums, for the cities
of the world—all
their joyful streets, all their terrors—
for the dead and the way
time shoves us along, ignoring every
protest. Cry child,
and let it be the song, trapped beneath
this flat bone,
here where my ribs come together.

## Iron

How strange to run out of iron,
to fill up with yawn.
A finger prick beads blood
not so red, not so thick.
How strange to sit in the cancer chair
and not have cancer, to lose
an hour watching a tube infuse
a pouch of coffee-brown solution
into the back of my needled hand
until the sack was shriveled, my avatar.
Done, my vein looked the same,
and I'd felt no pain sitting there
daydreaming of blood, bridles, needles,
true north, and the slow triumph of rust.

## Lucky You

All the breaks
you'll never know. Red light
that kept you from being
broadsided and brain-damaged
just three blocks further on.
The thief who would've broken
in and waited under your bed
with a gun, got killed
when he was only ten, a freak
accident that broke his neck.

The thunderstorm bruising
the horizon would've been my last,
but I was on the couch, too sick
to get up and check the car windows
when the pelting rain started
and the tree limb fell, busting
the sidewalk and burying
its splintered end deep in dirt.

What doesn't happen, doesn't
hurt—hurtles by like a city block-sized
mountain of rock silently shooting
past the earth, whizzes by unseen
like a stray bullet, like germs in a sneeze.

Another year of drinking that water
and the doctor would've said,
"I hate to break this to you."
Good thing the phone rang.
Good thing they took a wrong turn.
I'm so glad you came early. Oh,
and that mosquito you just slapped,
that was the one. Lucky you.

**Powerball**

The *Savior of World* got sold
for a fortune and that took me back
to the basement on Kenmore Street:
playing UNO at the Catholic Worker house—
cigarettes, coffee, and donuts—
with a half a dozen other losers like me.

It's a good painting, I like the hippie,
stoned look of him, the way he has
his right hand up as if he might flip us off
instead of offering that lukewarm
sign of peace, and the crystal orb
cupped in his left hand's a nice touch,
hinting that all the riches of the world
are nothing but an illusion of glass.

Four hundred and fifty million bucks, Jesus
that's a lot of money—Kardashian,
Raytheon, Gates, F-22 kind of money—
kind of money twelve million souls
dream of every Wednesday and Saturday
as five white, numbered balls roll,
followed by the red one—the Powerball
that bestows or withholds a life

of wealth. The Savior threatens, "Woe
to you who are rich, for you have
already received your comfort," though
Jussi Pylkkänen declares, "the piece
is, [*striking the gavel with spirit*] sold!"

## Rimsky-Korsakov's Bus

I liked driving the bus with Mozart
and his horns—a little fox hunt
down Clark Street and up Broadway
to the mental health center.
I liked driving the bus
in hectic traffic with Paganini:
all those stops, starts, swerves and passes.
I liked driving that blue bus
with its rust holes in the floor
and my little tinny radio on the dash.
I liked driving the bus with composers
and music I didn't even know—
that time I stopped to pick up clients
at the Stratford rooming house
with its two dead trees
and seven torn window screens.
Elizabeth, a forty year old Black woman
past the worst years
of her schizophrenia, stepped inside
and stopped beside me,
humming with her eyes closed,
humming along with the music on the radio.
Then she smiled and headed for a seat
sighing—almost singing—
"Oh *Scheherazade*,
I just love *Scheherazade*."

## The Arch

Forty-eight thousand tons of concrete and steel rise,
curving high into the air.
After twenty five years, here I am again
walking toward the gleaming St. Louis Arch
beside the clay colored Mississippi.
Forty-eight thousand tons—
as fathomable to me as the weight of the earth,
the space between the stars,
the stretch of the past. I measure
the past in inches, in rings, in memories.
The past curves and rises—an arch, a door.
Twenty five years ago six of us
walked this walkway to the arch.
The maples lining the way were small and spindly;
I could circle their trunks with my little hands.
My father said, "Think about it. Someday
when you're grown you'll come back
with your kids, and these trees will be big by then."
My sons hear this story and watch
as I try to circle one of the trees with my big hands—
too small now to make a ring
around the solid trunk. We look up
into the heights of leaves and shade.
For once my father was right. Standing
with my mother, he must have watched
my sisters and me running toward the arch,
then looked up and felt the weight
of his own years rising and bending
the way backbones bend, or legs bow
as we grow old. We grow old.

**Donuts**

Last night as temperatures spiraled
toward zero and winds swirled
snow, my thoughts circled back
a few years to a night in Minneapolis
when I did donuts with my little son.

It was in January, in an empty
parking lot covered with snow.
In our old black Volvo I turned
to my son and said, "Are you
buckled in? Here we go!"

Under cones of yellow-orange light
I turned the wheel and hit the gas.
We slid blurry circles across the night-
orange snow, laughing and yelling,
"Whoa! Whoa! Whoa!..."

Sometimes you want to give it a whirl,
put all the chips on red—or be a big zero,
a no-show when 8 a.m. rolls
around for work or school. The world
is always turning. I put my foot down

and turned the wheel hard—
a dozen loose and useless circles in the dark.

## Gabe's Teeth Again

Once more he cries out, stiffens
away, then settles back on me
moaning himself to sleep.

I used to get up at four-thirty every morning
to write for three hours.
I used to read for hours each day.
I used to sleep through the night.

But it's Gabe's teeth again,
cutting and hurting his gums.
On my chest he whimpers,
even in his sleep.

From my first son I learned
it takes more than a year
for all the teeth to cut through;
no one ever told me that.
Everything takes longer than I think.

How many mornings has it been?
And what do I have to show for it?
A mind that wanders.
A sheaf of poems.
The teeth in his mouth.

## Forty and Ten

The Arch was behind us,
the Mississippi below, and Illinois,
where we live, just ahead.
I was driving, and my son, Gabe,
had just fallen asleep beside me.
His beautiful face
was tilted down and toward me.
I steered us into the lane
that continued due east beyond the bridge.
I wish I could say that we—
forty and ten years old—
hung in a balance between
west and east, night and day,
ocean and ocean, wakefulness and sleep.
I wish I could say that
the wide river flowing below
carried some trace of our lives
a thousand miles down to the sea.
Truth is, the bridge was nothing
but a plain, old bridge—chipped concrete
and low, squared guard rails—
and the great, mud-colored river
was just a slow river going south
with boats and barges and a beautiful name.
But we're good enough,
and the miles of dull highway
and all the roads that brought us back—
to our town, to our small white house,
to the bicycles crowding the porch,
to the front door that opened for us—
were enough to make that river
more than just the dirty river that it is,
to make our crossing over more than just
leaving one state, and entering another.

**T-Rex**

When you're two
there's a dinosaur,
a ten foot *Tyrannosaurus*,
out in the country
standing in someone's yard
between a pond and the woods
and the nearby fields.

Strapped in your car seat,
you point and clap.
It's there all summer:
hot noons, thunderstorms,
sunflowers and butterflies.
Come fall its teeth
are still bared
as flowers shrivel,
leaves turn yellow and red.
Even in winter it stands there
with its small front claws
and a cake of snow
on its wide, flat fiberglass head.

Come spring, when you're three,
it's gone. Where, oh where?
It's gone. You're three.
It's gone forever.

## Field with Pheasants

Squawks like rusty springs,
old hinges. It's spring at last
in the withered, winter grass:
*rasp, rasp.* Soon one ups
and lowflies for what it wants.

Though birdlust wings the field,
one man walks downcast
as if clocks only go *tick-tock,*
*tick-tock,* as if every eyehole
is laced and every button holds
forever the lip of the buttonhole.

I hear the desire, birdcry
from down low in the meadow,
then watch it flap and fly.
What are feathers for?
That other fellow never looks up.

I refuse to be gloomed
by far off November
when triggers will be pulled,
and bodies will fall to earth.

## Coyotes

Coming back, I was high in the air
though my father had just been buried
a few days after his and my mother's
forty-sixth anniversary. I'd changed
planes in St. Louis—that Arch, that river—
and rectangles of farmland below
were bare and brown. Early November.
The plane descended toward our town,
but didn't land—circled once, then again.
The captain announced that coyotes
were on the runway, and we'd land
once they were out of the way.
With my face against the little window
as we banked and turned, I watched
half a dozen lean ghosts disappear
into the tall grass below.

## Sleepers

Is it coming? It is
more than a hundred tons
of rods, pistons, fuel and wheels—
like a spoonful of black hole
dragging the weight of
the world. Sheathed in steel,
it crosses the plains with white light
in the lead punching a hole
in night's black hide like an awl,
like a bullet through a wall. It's pulling
corn syrup and crude oil and people
and acid and nuts and bolts and God
knows what else. We shuffle stare
and mutter something like prayer
as it goes by. Whoosh, roar, rumble—
it ignores us, rolling on rails endless
as math, shiny as dimes. "The past
is the past," I tell my boys, but keep
my fears of what's coming to myself.
There will be trainloads of time
for them to draw their own conclusions.
What do I know anyway?
After it passes, we—nothing
to the machinery, the turning, whirring
gears and shafts—turn away.
Is it gone? It is
that spot of red blinking dimmer
in the distance. That's the end
of it pulling away. Another weight
pulls us home to bed, to maybe
nightmares, maybe dreams.

## Solids

I hold beginnings,
first taste
of what earth offers.
In a spoon no bigger
than my little finger
I bring him his first
solid food:
rice mush
with apple puree.
Legs kick
and arms lift.
His hunger is intimate
with his little body—
forthright and undistracted.
Such pure want. If only
I could remember.
But I can give,
can feed my boy.
Mouthful by mouthful
he tastes and swallows,
and is satisfied. How it begins.

## Skies

Be generous with fiery, purple
endings and the delicate, elegant
glitter of stars. Beneath sky lies
harder sky—fields of corn and beans
to the far edge of everywhere.
Long gone are heavens of high grass,
starry with yellow, purple, pink and white.

And sometimes I've glimpsed it—
in a coyote sprinting in, then out of
the headlights; or in a deer midair
leaping a fence before disappearing into
the trees—the third sky, the one wanting
answers: *Where are you going,*
*and just who do you think you are?*

## Twist

With the first I hesitated
at the moment of twisting,
and threw it, head half off,
into the river. The next one
I held hard, while quick-wristed
I snapped it in two
like a fresh green bean.
My mother taught me
how to kill shrimp:
one deft twist
severs the body we keep
from the head that's tossed
like an offering
back to the brackish river.
She also taught me
the net in the teeth,
the way the body twists,
then uncoils—spreading
the weighted edge out
into an arc of release
and plunge to the water.
She showed me the pulling-in
with live shrimp tangled
in the net's small weave.
But she did not tell me, "Remember.
Remember." That was joy:
the body living and moving
through time. That was the muse
and her endless lust
for memory and words:
salty rag taste of the net,
beefy smell of the mealy bait,
muddy shine of the shrimp,
and splash of the net striking the water.

## Fireflies

Night falls dark as new, blue
denim, and fireflies dot the yard
with yellow-green sparks.
They're seeking mates,
but my boys are watching, too;
hunt them with tennis rackets.
The two of them chase and swing
at every blink of light they see.
When they hit one, it falls
in small glowing streaks
like a little plane shot down,
like a dim shooting star.
I remember killing
dragonflies with a stick,
slicing them in midair, cutting
them to pieces where they landed.
I remember shooting ants
with rubber bands, and nailing crabs
with shells at low tide.
But now I hate killing anything,
even cockroaches. I hate
fishing—the way the worm twists
and lashes when I stick the tip
of the hook up and into
its gooey, boneless body;
the way the fish stares in silence
as I tear the barb out of its mouth.
I'd rather let every living thing
live. I'd rather be like the fireflies:
all light and desire, turning and flashing
midair. Blink. Blink. Blink.

## Box Turtles Fucking

Hurry, come see. He
was standing on his stubby back legs,
the concave shell of his yellow belly
pressed snug to the round rock
of her dark back.
We knew.
His little front feet were scrabbling
for a hold. His neck
was extended, stretched taut
and pulling a look of pure
lust on his face that made us—
thirteen and fourteen— laugh and snort.

We'd never seen two turtles doing it,
but there they were. Man,
he was jazzed and desperate
like he'd taken a baited hook
in the beak and was being hauled
up by the face, all that urge
dragging him out of his shell,
tugging him to stand and grimace
and grab on. We'd read somewhere
that sometimes the male will fall
backwards when he's done,
and stuck on his back like that, will die.

I could live with that;
though I figured it'd be a long time
before I'd get so hooked. Sometimes
it seemed the want and wait
would drive me nuts.
God knows
those turtles were caught up
in the sheer, raw draw of it.
I might've watched and grown
hushed, like someone bedside
at a death or a birth. Oh, I did watch,
and watch, but like the dumb fuck
I was, all I managed to do was laugh.

## Steam

First time.  Nothing
like imagined.
Her below me.
Her above me.
Her hair in my eyes.
My hair in her fingers.
An album turning,
"Who shall I say is calling?"
I will tell my sons
it was like *this*.
It was sun through thin blinds.
It was cold air
sliding in under warm.
It was God turning to steam,
then nothing.
It was the wet nakedness of tongues.
I will tell my sons
because I have no daughters.
I will tell them I have nothing
to be ashamed of.
I will tell them it was
the end of faith,
the beginning of wisdom;
was everything and nothing at once.

## Watermelon

Clothes to fold, floor
to sweep, and checks to sign
before we sleep—
you place it on the table.
Holding a foot-long knife,
you turn the melon, eyeing
its dark green striations,
its pale, fishy belly.
Then you find the spot,
force in the blade and pull,
splitting the melon lengthwise.
Then you halve the halves,
and again until there are eight
green wedges like longboats
loaded with wet, red fruit.
Ten-thirty, chores still to do
and beads of sweat trickling
like little insects down the neck,
you sit down to carve and eat
the reddest, sweetest pieces
from just above the rows
of black and abundant seeds.
Juice drips from your fingertips,
bleeds down your chin. Wife,
you sit there like a calm god
sampling a sacrifice—calf's loin
or lamb's shank—like Love
victorious, savoring the sweet
red meat of the heart.

## Setting the Table

1.

I don't give a shit for the frivolous: Get to the point.
Cut to the chase. Thin steel, I've got an edge.
Fork brags fingers, and spoon fancies itself
mouth's smooth lover, life's shiny mirror,
but in a tight spot—trapped in a back room,
a dead end street—what would you want
to pull from your pocket, to bet your sweet life on?

2.

First there was my bloody cousin who knows
where the heart hides, where skin rips red and wet
from muscled flesh. I came after knife; we are
a lot alike: sharp points, hearts of steel. But he
is like the tyrant's mind or the slanderer's tongue,
while I am an extra hand—for harvests, for feasts—
easy with arm in arm, at home among plates of food.

3.

I am the smooth one—cupped hand, smallest bowl.
If it can spill, fill me with it; I'll carry it. I am shaped
for the mouth as centering for a dome. Tongues
turn me over and lips caress me as I slip out
empty and clean as a mirror. You can praise
knife: thin guile, bloody edge. You can admire
fork's four stiff prongs. But when it spills or drips,
when lovers lie down—breast pressed to back,
buttocks to hips—the word that is spoken is *spoon*.

## Slugs

> "Never to despise in myself what I have been taught
> to despise. Nor to despise the other."
> —Muriel Rukeyser, from "Despisals"

Salted, burned, hacked,
poisoned, smashed, drowned.
With the sharp edge of a shovel,
under the blunt weight of my heel,
I too have killed quite a few.

Shame: what is slick and sticky,
what tastes and smells
of the sea, of sex:
mollusk tang, salty come.
Disgust for the primal,
slippery urge: semen, slug slime.

My mother and father never
told me one word about sex,
not penis, vulva, or intercourse.
Even in private probably
never said dick, pussy, or fuck.
Oh shame, don't speak it;
don't dare say its name.

So here I am this afternoon
seeking slugs, to make peace.
I find and follow a silver trail
across leaves and dirt
until it comes to a slug
asleep beneath a log.

It is breathing, glistening,
moist with clear mucous.
Sticky, slimy, nasty, gross
are in my mind, but
I make myself touch it,
pick it up with my bare hands.

I lift it for a closer look
and watch it on my palm
as it stirs and extends itself.
Its two little feelers
barely brush my skin,
while the specks of its eyes
rise and sway at the tips
of its erect and delicate horns.

It doesn't know what I am,
how many I've killed.
Oozing and unafraid
it mouths and muscles its way
along the lines of my palm.
Look at it, stretched across my hand
like a man's little penis after he comes:
small, moist and half-hard.
And look at me, tender
for a slug, tender
to give myself forgiveness.